1975

AMERICAN
PRIMITIVE

"I am ashamed of the age I live in."
John Adams

AMERICAN PRIMITIVE

THE WORDS OF
John & Abigail Adams

put into a sequence for the theater,
with addenda in rhyme by

WILLIAM GIBSON

ATHENEUM *NEW YORK*

1972

Composition by Brown Bros. Linotypers, Inc., New York City
Printed and bound by Halliday Lithograph Corporation,
Hanover, Massachusetts
Designed by Harry Ford
First Edition

T O

JOHN ADAMS

FOR THE PLEASURE OF HIS COMPANY

THE TEXT *which follows embodies a concept of staging which is play-like; it is one way of presenting this material. Obviously the text is not a "play"—it is eyewitness history, it is self-portraits by two of our parents, it is our birth certificate—and its nature lends itself to varied means of presentation. It would interest me if directors made free with it also as recital, or backed it with projections, or interwove it with music and dance.*

INDISPENSABLE *in my presentation, however, is the active use of a great backdrop map, upon which the military moves of the times will be legible to all. Changes in the map may be effected in any suitable manner, from projections to actors hanging up symbols, but to mark and follow them is imperative. The geographical ignorance of most of us cannot be overstated—half of our actors in auditions had not heard of and could not pronounce Ticonderoga—but the need is also dramaturgic. The psychological progression in the text is minimal; what progresses is the military peril overhanging the participants, and it must be made clear to the eye.*

W. G.

Cast

JOHN
ABIGAIL

3 MEN

3 WOMEN

1 BOY

1 GIRL

ACT I, 1774–75
ACT II, 1776–77

In and near the cities of Boston and Philadelphia.

AMERICAN PRIMITIVE *was first presented—under another title—by the Berkshire Theatre Festival, in Stockbridge, Massachusetts, in July, 1969; it starred Anne Bancroft and James Broderick, and was directed by Frank Langella.*

In revised form it was next presented by the Circle in the Square at Ford's Theatre, in Washington, D.C., in January, 1971, starring Salome Jens and Michael Higgins, directed by Theodore Mann.

ACT I

House lights on.

The ACTORS *in their everyday clothes—there is to be no attempt at verisimilitude in costume, merely the use of whatever scraps will identify roles momentarily— come onstage to prepare the platforms, stools, props;* THEY *wait in position.*

WOMAN 1 *comes down front.*

WOMAN 1: The dialogue you will hear tonight was written by John and Abigail Adams. It has been put together from their letters, diaries, books; the words they speak are theirs.

MAN 1: The rhymes of course are not.

(House lights start down, stage lights steal in, music may commence; the transition into stage lighting should be unnoticeable.)

MAN 3:
We begin with the tea
In '73—

WOMAN 2:

> The bay all afloat—

> (*A cannonshot blow on a kettledrum scatters the* GROUP; MAN 2 *takes position as a* BRITISH SENTRY *with musket, his stance stylized, as in an old engraving.*)

MAN 2:

> Boston port is shut down!

WOMAN 3:

> Redcoats at every wharf and street,
> An occupied town—

MAN 1:

> And our fathers,
> That rabble, forbidden to meet,
> Vote—

MAN 3:

> A motion!

> (*The drum convokes the* ACTORS *upstage center; except for* JOHN *and* ABIGAIL, *their moves and groupings may be ritualistic, half-dance, and speeches assigned hereafter to "*MEN, WOMEN*" are meant to be distributed among single voices as above.*
> MAN 3 *reads them a document.*)

MAN 3: "It is highly expedient and necessary that a meeting of the several colonies of this continent

be had, to consult upon the miseries to which
they are reduced by certain acts of Parliament—"

(JOHN *comes out of the* GROUP, *saddle bag in
hand; the* GROUP *remain on.*)

JOHN: A Congress. It is to be a school of political
prophets, I suppose, a nursery of American states-
men.

(HE *drops the bag, sits on a platform edge to jot
the following in a notebook.*)

I feel myself unequal to this business. I have four
children; every lawyer grows rich who engages on
the side of the crown—

(*The* GROUP *separates from* ABIGAIL, *seated with
her* CHILDREN *as in an early painting.*

The MAP *shows Boston, with Braintree just south
of it.*)

We have not men fit for the times. I am melancholy for the public, and anxious for my family.

ABIGAIL (*Writing*): Braintree, August 15th, 1774. My
dearest friend—

(*Their communication is writing; this made clear,*

SHE *will speak directly to him, and* HE *to her, whenever possible.*)

I know not where this will find you, whether upon the road or in Philadelphia.

JOHN (*Writing*): I am at a loss, totally at a loss, what to do when we get there.

ABIGAIL (*Writing*): We are burnt up with the drouth. My poor cows will certainly petition you, informing you they have been deprived of their ancient privileges—

(SHE *is teasing, thinks better of it.*)

Your task is difficult and important; and that which at all times and in all places attends you is the most affectionate regard of your Abigail Adams.

(SHE *rises, passes close to him.*)

Excuse this very bad writing, if you had mended my pen it would have been better, once more adieu.

(SHE *pauses to gaze at the* SENTRY; JOHN *with the notebook in hand calls after her.*)

JOHN: I keep a journal which shall be your entertainment when I come home. Your wandering—John Adams.

(THEY *retire; the* OTHERS *come down, set a plat-form and props, speak.*)

MEN, WOMEN:

You know the type, on the make,
Town lawyer, family, farm in the outskirts,
You are the type. Be comfy,
Don't do what hurts.

What kind of people not like us did it take?

Look at the country, this is the theme,
The gangrene of cities in it:
We are the kind who end a dream.

What kind begin it?

(THEY *separate;* ABIGAIL *mounts the platform as a hill.*)

ABIGAIL: I feel not a little agitated with the accounts I have this day from Boston, of a plot—the King's General Gage to seize our province's stock of powder. This has so enraged our people that great commotions have arisen; General Gage is mounting cannon upon Beacon Hill, digging entrenchments, throwing up breastworks—

(*The* MAP *enlarges to show both Boston and Philadelphia, the coastline and cities between.*)

JOHN (*Down, gazing at sights*): A number of carriages
     and gentlemen came out of Philadelphia to meet
     us—the most active sons of liberty—

     (HE *turns to a* TRIO *of* MEN *with fingers on lips.*)

MAN 1: You must not utter the word independence.
MAN 2: Nor give the least hint of the idea, in Congress
     or—
MAN 3: Independence is as unpopular as the Stamp Act
     itself.
JOHN (*Uncertain*): I believe we shall agree on non-
     importation of British goods?

     (THEY *go upstage, talking.*)

ABIGAIL: I am very impatient to receive a letter from
     you.
JOHN (*Alarmed*): The bombardment of Boston?

     (HE *wheels,* ABIGAIL *descends to* WOMEN.)

     My dear, we have a confused account of a catas-
     trophe—

     (*A buzz among the* MEN *calls him back.*)

     My babes are never out of my mind—
ABIGAIL (*Turns*): Everyone I see is inquiring after you,
     and when did I hear. All my intelligence is from
     the newspaper, and I saw by that that you arrived.

JOHN (*Relieved*): No blood spilled, but General Gage has taken away the provincial powder at Cambridge.

ABIGAIL: Five weeks have passed, and not one line have I received.

JOHN: Let us eat potatoes and drink water, rather than submit.

(MEN 1 & 2 *bring him a chair and a desk piled with papers;* HE *sits, while the* OTHERS *create a suggestion of a hall with a royal flag and lectern with gavel.*)

ABIGAIL: We are all well here.

(SHE *sits on a platform near him, chatty.*)

Sunday evening there passed by here about two hundred sons of liberty and marched down to the powder house, from which they took the powder. The reason was that we had so many Tories here they dare not trust us with it. The church parson thought they were coming after him and ran up garret, they say; another jumped out of his window and hid among the corn.

(SHE *yearns toward him, wanting to touch him.*)

I hope you will find means to convey me some intelligence—

JOHN: I wish I could write to you a dozen times every
     day. But—

     (HE *leaves her, to study the audience.*)

     I had the characters and views of fifty gentlemen,
     total strangers to me, to study, and the trade,
     policy, and whole interest of a dozen provinces to
     learn, when I came here.

     (ABIGAIL *rises to receive a letter from* WOMAN 3;
     JOHN *turns back to his pile of papers.*)

     I have multitudes of pamphlets, newspapers, and
     letters to read, plans of policy to consider—
ABIGAIL: They met me at the door with your letter. It
     really gave me such a flow of spirits that I was not
     composed enough to sleep till one o'clock.
JOHN: The Congress is assembling.

     (*The* MEN *mutter at rear.*)

     When it first met, a motion that it should be
     opened with prayer was opposed, because we were
     so divided in religious sentiments. Mr. Samuel
     Adams arose and said he was no bigot—
MAN 3 (*Halfway down*): I am no bigot, and can hear a
     prayer from any gentleman of piety who is a friend
     to his country.

JOHN: Next morning an episcopal clergyman read the collect for the day.

(*The* GIRL *brings* ABIGAIL *an opened Bible.*)

I beg you to read that Psalm.

(ABIGAIL *reads to the* GIRL.)

ABIGAIL:

    O Lord, fight against them that fight against me,
    Stop the way against them;
    Let them be confounded, let them be turned back,
    Let them be as chaff before the wind;
    And all my bones shall say, Lord, who is like unto thee?

JOHN: We were guilty of a masterly stroke in moving an *episcopal* clergyman read prayers, it has had a very good effect.

(ABIGAIL *gives the Bible back to the* GIRL.)

ABIGAIL: If we expect the blessings of our fathers, we should return a little more to their primitive simplicity of manners.

JOHN: There is in the Congress a collection of the greatest men upon this continent. Here are fortunes, abilities, eloquence equal to any; here is a— diversity of religions, educations, interests, such as it would seem impossible to unite in one plan of conduct, non-importation of British goods.

(ABIGAIL *comes down front, in a bonnet.*)

ABIGAIL: Boston. I called here to see this much injured town—invaded with fleets and armies, the courts of justice shut, our commerce totally ruined, thousands reduced to want.

(MAN 3 *sounds gavel.*)

JOHN: Debates.

MAN 1 (*Right*): Connecticut exports 30,000 bushels of flaxseed, no loss to stop, the seed may be made into oil, we have many oil mills.

MAN 2 (*Left*): South Carolina exports 150,000 barrels of rice, 300 ships employed, to stop it would cost all our trade!

JOHN (*Impatient*): Fifty strangers, jealous of each other—

ABIGAIL: The Negroes got up a petition to General Gage telling him they would fight for the King, provided *he* would liberate them. I wish there was not a slave in the province. It always appeared a most iniquitous scheme to me, to fight ourselves for what we are daily robbing from those who have as good a right to freedom as we.

JOHN: We have numberless prejudices to remove here.

ABIGAIL (*Turns*): My mother has been low. You will receive a letter—

(SHE *gives it to him.*)

—from one as earnest to write to Papa as if the welfare of a kingdom depended upon it.

JOHN (*Opens it*): Tedious indeed is our business, slow as snails—

(HE *reads it; the* BOY *is silhouetted on a rear platform.*)

BOY: Sir. I have been trying ever since you went away to learn to write you a letter. I shall make poor work of it, but, sir, Mama says my duty to you may be expressed in poor writing as well as good. We all long to see you. I hope I grow a better boy and that you will have no occasion to be ashamed of me. I am, sir, your dutiful son, John Quincy Adams.

(JOHN *is moved by the letter;* ABIGAIL *waits behind him.*)

ABIGAIL: Many have been the anxious hours I have spent —and it looks as though the curtain was but just drawn and only the first scene disclosed, and whether the end will be tragical—

JOHN (*Jots in notebook*): Attended my duty upon the committee all day.

(HE *is restive, between the letter, the pile of papers, the notebook.*)

ABIGAIL: You cannot be, I know, nor do I wish to see you, an inactive spectator, but if the sword is drawn I bid adieu to all domestic felicity.

JOHN (*More restive, jots*): Attended my duty upon committees, nibbling and quibbling.

ABIGAIL: I venture to write most anything in this letter, because I know the bearer. I envy him, that he should see you before I do.

JOHN (*Jots*): Attended my duty all day on the subcommit—

(HE *slaps down, is out of his chair.*)

I am wearied to death with the life I lead!

(HE *comes to address the audience.*)

This assembly is like no other that ever existed. Every man in it is a great man, an orator, a critic, a statesman—and upon every question must *show* his oratory, his criticism, and his political abilities! If it was moved that three and two make five we should be entertained with logic, law, history, politics and mathematics for two whole days!

(HE *turns up, comes back.*)

And then pass it unanimously!

(HE *marches upstage to confer with the* MEN, *who reassure him;* ABIGAIL *sits in his chair, touches his papers.*)

ABIGAIL: My much loved friend. I dare not express to you how ardently I long for your return. The idea plays about my heart, awakens all the tender sentiments that years have increased, the whole collected stock will break forth and—

JOHN (*Back*): My dear, this was one of the happiest days of my life. There is no idea of submission here in anybody's head; America will support the Massachusetts or perish with her.

ABIGAIL: You will burn these letters lest they fall from your pocket, and expose your most affectionate friend.

JOHN: We agree on non-importation. You must keep these letters; they may exhibit to our posterity a kind of picture of these times.

(MAN 1 *sounds the gavel,* HE *turns to it.* ABIGAIL *leaves his chair to join the* CHILDREN.)

This day the Congress finished. It is not very likely that I shall ever see this part of the world again.

(HE *collects his papers.* MAN 1 *comes to give him two or three coins.*)

MAN 1 : Twelve shillings.

(*The* OTHERS *come down, removing the papers, desk, chair, rearranging a platform;* JOHN *contemplates the coins in his hand.*)

MEN, WOMEN (*As* THEY *work*):
Twelve shillings a day
In '74
Was a delegate's pay.

Well, it kept
The wolf from the door
Of a room upstairs where he slept
Alone,
Too poor for a house, and was never known
To be faithless.

It kept
The man from the wife. Except
It went a long ways
When he rode in the saddle for thirteen days
To be with her once more,
Content
Within sight and scent
Of the incoming sea

And war.

(THEY *separate, leaving* JOHN *still with the coins, his family now seated behind him; the* GIRL *brings him a clay pipe.* HE *sits with them, relaxed.*)

JOHN: I am determined to avoid public life. I have neither fortune, leisure, nor genius for it.

ABIGAIL (*Sewing*): There is nothing so much to render a man fractious as living without females about him.

JOHN: I bid farewell to great affairs. I had rather chop wood and make fences on my little farm—

(*Interruption by a rattle of drums, musketfire, a scream; the lights change,* ABIGAIL *shepherds the* CHILDREN *to safety,* JOHN *moves upstage amidst a possible mime of* REDCOATS *and* MINUTEMEN.

The MAP *shows the Boston area, with Lexington and Concord; the British arrow pointed at them pulls back into Boston, which is then ringed by arrows representing* MINUTEMEN *from all directions.*)

MEN, WOMEN:
Lexington and Concord!

A raid for powder
But not as planned:
The redcoats fall back into Boston town,

Farmers
Muskets and pitchforks in hand
Pour in, dig in,
Fifteen thousand dig in to stand
Bristling,
A human fence round the city!

The word like a fire is loose in the land!

(ABIGAIL *mounts the platform as a hill,* JOHN *comes below her in a hurry with a parcel.*)

JOHN: Connecticut is raising six thousand men, Rhode Island fifteen hundred, New York has seized the customs house, arms, ammunition, to stand by the Congress. I have no doubts now of the union!

ABIGAIL: I endeavor to be very heroic—

JOHN: My duty to your mother, and a thousand thanks for her cake.

(HE *starts upstage with it unwanted, stops.*)

ABIGAIL: —yet my heart feels like lead—

JOHN (*Back*): Write me whether my brothers intend to take a command in the army. I won't advise them, but they should apply to Dr. Warren soon.

(HE *hurries upstage;* WOMEN 1 & 2 *set the desk near* ABIGAIL.)

ABIGAIL (*Warning him*): The British have a list of all
those they call obnoxious; they and their effects—

(SHE *descends.*)

—are to suffer destruction.

(SHE *sits on the platform, to the desk;* SHE *writes,
in some conflict.*)

To Joseph Warren, president, Provincial Assembly.
Sir, a brother of Mr. Adams, Elihu, is desirous of
joining the army; he requested me to write you.
He is a person both of steadiness and probity—

(*The big bell is struck,* SHE *stops, the* WOMEN *in
shawls and the* CHILDREN *flock around her in a
flurry of voices.*)

WOMEN, CHILDREN (*Calling*):
Three British sloops
In the bay—

One cutter—

Bound
For the island—

Three hundred troops
Stealing
The hay—

ABIGAIL: People, women, children, flocking down this
way—

WOMEN: Stop them—

ABIGAIL: The expedition is to the Island, for hay for the
British horses—

(SHE *is calling to* JOHN, *though* HE *is out of sight.*)

Our men put off for the island, the enemy decamped, our people set fire to the hay, with the
barn—

(*The* GROUP *becomes refugees; when* SHE *rises,* ONE
or TWO *are at her feet.*)

Our house has been in confusion, the recruits
coming in for lodging, for supper; refugees from
Boston seek asylum for a day, a night, a week—

(JOHN *with papers mounts the platform as his
room, contemplates it.*)

You can hardly imagine how we live.

JOHN: Philadelphia, where bastards and legislators are
begotten.

(HE *sits as on a bed, takes off a shoe, pinches his
eyes;* ABIGAIL *wanders in her house, not turning
when* JOHN *speaks.*)

ABIGAIL: This day month you set off. I want to know
how you do, how you stood your journey, how
are your eyes—

JOHN: I have found this Congress like the last, our
business hazardous, our deliberations tedious.

ABIGAIL (*Waits*): You don't say one word about your
health.

JOHN: I have had miserable health and blind eyes, yet
I keep about.

ABIGAIL (*Waits*): Though my letters have less merit,
they have more words.

(SHE *returns among the refugees to the desk, to
find letters.*)

JOHN (*Vexed*): We find a great many bundles of weak
nerves; Mr. Dickinson must have a *new* petition to
the King. This measure of imbecility I dread like
death.

Colonel Washington appears in his uniform.

ABIGAIL (*Turns now*): You inquire who were at the
engagement at the Island—all of Braintree who
were able to bear arms. Your younger brother Elihu
was one of the first.

(JOHN *twists to listen, gazing at the refugees.*)

He is very desirous of being in the army but your
good mother is violent against it; neither he nor I
dare let her know he is trying for a place.

JOHN: Dr. Warren writes me about my brother.
ABIGAIL: Gage's proclamation you will receive—

(*A drum roll;* JOHN *listens to* MAN 1 *as a British* SENTRY *reads a proclamation to the huddled* WOMEN.)

MAN 1: "The infatuated multitudes have long suffered themselves to be conducted by certain well-known incendiaries and traitors—"
JOHN (*Rises*): Traitors—
MAN 1: "—in a fatal progression of crimes—"

(MAN 2 *sounds gavel.*)

MAN 2: A motion—for a second petition to the King—
JOHN (*Interrupting*): Juvenilities become not a great assembly like this.

(HE *comes down,* MEN 1 & 3 *bring the desk to him,* HE *stands by it.*)

I entreat the attention of all the members—

(THEY *retire, inattentive;* HE *speaks to the country outside the room.*)

—and of all the continent! The case of Massachusetts is the most urgent, but it cannot be long

before every colony must follow. When the sword
is drawn, throw away the scabbard!

(*With increasing boldness.*)

The first step is to recommend to every province
to seize on all the crown officers and hold them as
hostages, for the security of the people of Boston;
and to institute governments for themselves, under
their own authority; and immediately to adopt the
army in Cambridge as a *continental* army—to appoint a general, and take upon ourselves the pay,
subsistence, and munitions of the troops—

(*Defiant.*)

—to declare the colonies free, sovereign, and *independent states!*—and to inform Great Britain we
are willing to seek the friendship of her enemies,
France and—

(MAN 2 *at rear hisses;* JOHN *breaks off.*)

I see horror and detestation on some counte-
nances—

ABIGAIL: Nabby has enclosed a letter to you, would
excuse the writing because of a sore thumb she has.

(*The* GIRL *brings it to* JOHN, HE *speaks hurriedly
over his shoulder.*)

JOHN: My dear child, your pretty letter gives me pleasure, both as a token of your affection and of your improvement in handwriting—

(HE *wheels with it to* MAN 2.)

In my opinion, powder and artillery are the most infallible *conciliatory* measures we can adopt!

(*The* GIRL *runs back, the* BOY *is seated at* ABIGAIL's *skirt.*)

ABIGAIL: You would laugh to see them all run upon the sight of a letter, like chickens when the hen clucks. And Charles with open mouth—
BOY: What did Pa say, did not he write no more?

(JOHN *pauses over the letter in his hand, very worried;* ABIGAIL *gathers the* CHILDREN.)

JOHN (*To himself*): My dear Nabby, Johnny, and Tommy, come here and kiss me.
ABIGAIL: Every town is filled with the refugees from Boston. We now expect our sea coasts ravaged. My heart beats at every whistle I hear.
JOHN (*To himself*): Full of anxieties, apprehending daily—news from Boston—

(MAN 3 *brings his papers from the platform to the desk.*)

ABIGAIL: Courage I know we have in abundance, conduct I hope we shall not want, but powder, where shall we get?

JOHN: The dangers that surround us!—

(HE *and* MAN 3 *pace, talking;* ABIGAIL *stands near the huddled* WOMEN.)

—not only the petition, but a Southern party, jealous of a New Engand army under a New England general—

MAN 3: What shall we do?

JOHN: Take a step to compel our colleagues to declare themselves!

ABIGAIL: Did ever any kingdom regain its liberty, once invaded, without bloodshed?

(MAN 3 *sounds gavel;* JOHN *turns back to the desk, arm raised.*)

JOHN: I rise with a motion to adopt the army and appoint a general; I have but one gentleman in my mind—a gentleman from Virginia!

MAN 3: Second the motion!

(ABIGAIL *walks with the* CHILDREN, *as in an orchard.*)

ABIGAIL: Tis a fine growing season, having had a charming rain; your meadow is fit to mow—

MEN 1 *& * 2 (*Sound gavel*): Postponed!

JOHN (*Scathing*): The human mind is not naturally the
clearest atmosphere.

(HE *gathers some of his papers.*)

ABIGAIL: Fruit promises well, but the caterpillars have
been innumerable.

JOHN: Pains must be taken—

(HE *and* MAN 3 *caucus with the* MEN *upstage.*)

ABIGAIL: I have devoted one hour to you, I daresay you
are not in debt. Breakfast calls—

(JOHN *hurries up the platform as into his room,
speaks after her as* SHE *retires.*)

JOHN: My dear, the Congress have made choice of the
modest, virtuous, and brave George Washington,
Esquire, to be the general of the American army!

(ABIGAIL *is out of sight; from the percussion a
cheery military sound, drums and fife;* JOHN *sits
alone, sorry for himself.*)

I, worn out with scribbling for my bread and my
liberty, must leave others to wear the laurels I have
sown. Oh, that I was a soldier! I will be, I am reading military books.

Remember me to my dear brother—

(*The military sound alters, the kettledrum thunders
like cannon, the lights change; the* WOMEN *scream
over the roar,* ABIGAIL *stumbles down front in
horror.*

The MAP *shows Boston harbor and across the
water Charlestown and Bunker Hill; a British arrow
thrusts to break out of the ring.*)

ABIGAIL: The day, perhaps the decisive day, is come:
Charlestown is laid in ashes! The battle began upon
Bunker's Hill Saturday morning and has not ceased
yet, the constant roar of the cannon is so distressing
that we cannot eat, drink, or sleep—

(*A hush, and a great burning lights the stage.*)

I have just heard that our dear friend Dr. Warren
is no more, but fell fighting.

(SHE *goes to her knees.*)

Almighty God, cover the heads of our countrymen,
and be a shield to our friends.

JOHN (*Above, whispers*): A report of a battle, we wait
to hear more—

ABIGAIL (*Unbelieving*): The place of my fathers'
sepulchres lieth in waste, consumed with fire,

scarcely one stone remaineth upon another. We stand astonished that our people were not all cut off, their numbers did not exceed eight hundred, the reinforcements not able to get to them, and they had not half ammunition enough—the town in flames around them, the heat from the flames so intense as scarcely to be borne, the wind blowing the smoke all around them—

(*The burning fades.*)

Our prisoners were brought over to the Long Wharf and there laid all night without any care of their wounds; our friend Warren was thrown into the earth with many bodies over him.

(*The* WOMEN *mourn in a low keening;* ABIGAIL *rises to round fiercely on* JOHN *above.*)

Does every member feel for us? Do they realize what we suffer?

JOHN (*Slowly*): It is not so easy a thing for the most powerful state to conquer a country a thousand leagues off—

ABIGAIL: Your petitioning the King again pleases, forgive me if I say, the timid and the weak!

(SHE *strikes the papers off his desk;* SHE *stands to control her anger.*)

JOHN (*Harsh*): Burn our seaport towns, what then?

ABIGAIL: Not all the destruction they made has wounded me like the death of Warren.

JOHN: Will the King be nearer his mark after he has burned a beautiful town and murdered thirty thousand innocent people?

ABIGAIL: Those lines of Collins' continually sound in my ears—

How sleep the brave who sink to rest,
By all their country's wishes blest?

JOHN: Courage, my dear.

(THEY *stand unmoving.*)

WOMEN:

Bunker Hill,
The British are bled.

Who paid the bill?
Half of their soldiers
Wounded or dead
Litter the hillside, litter the beach
Like fingers dropped
From a bloody hand:
Boys, boys—

And the rabble still
Hang on, like a leech.

Washington rides in to take command.

(JOHN *comes down to the desk, picks up the papers;*
MAN 3 *brings the chair.*)

JOHN (*To Abigail*): I will tell you in future, but you
    shall keep it secret, a complete history of the be-
    havior of my compatriots—But we have a number
    of new and ingenious members. Mr. Jefferson seizes
    upon my heart.
    I am happy to hear my brother behaved well.
ABIGAIL (*Numb*): They had not half ammunition
    enough.
JOHN (*To* MAN 3): There are three powder mills in this
    province, two in New York, but no nitre. Cannot
    the Massachusetts begin to prepare both?
ABIGAIL: I am brave upon the whole; if danger comes
    near my dwelling I suppose I shall shudder.

(SHE *crosses to the* GIRL, *who waits with letters.*
MAN 3 *sounds the gavel.*)

JOHN (*Jots in notebook*): Voted! That two million
    dollars be issued in bills of credit; that ten com-
    panies of riflemen be sent to our army in Boston—
ABIGAIL: I have paper from you, I wish it had been
    more covered. All seem to be wrote in so much
    haste, they let me know that you exist, but some
    of them contain scarcely six lines.
JOHN: My dear, I have received your favors; they con-
    tain more particulars than any letters I had from
    anybody, full of useful information—

ABIGAIL *(Turns)*: I want some—sentimental effusions
of the heart. Are they all absorbed in the great
public? Being part of the whole, I lay claim to a
greater share than I have had. Johnny—Johnny
says—

BOY: Do you think Papa has so many things to do that
he will forget me?

(A silence. JOHN *is stricken by this;* ABIGAIL *takes
the* BOY *to her.)*

JOHN *(Low)*: My anxiety about you and the children,
as well as the country, has been extreme.

ABIGAIL: I must not grumble, I know your time is not
yours, nor mine.

*(*SHE *sends the* BOY *upstage.)*

As to Boston, I heard yesterday their beef is all
spent, all the fresh provisions they are obliged to
give to the sick and wounded. I hope we shall not
now have famine added to war.

JOHN *(Very patient)*: The business I have had upon my
mind has been as important as can be entrusted to
one man, and the intricacy of it is prodigious.

*(*ABIGAIL *mounts the platform as her bedroom;*
JOHN *handles his papers, evidencing one after
another.)*

When fifty men have a constitution to form, a
country of fifteen hundred miles extent to fortify,
a standing army of twenty-seven thousand men to
raise, pay, victual, and officer, numerous tribes of
Indians to negotiate with—

ABIGAIL: Next Wednesday is thirteen weeks since you
went away; every line from that far country is
precious.

JOHN: We *have* taken measures for powder which I
hope to explain to you—in person—

ABIGAIL (*Sits as in bed*): I do not feel easy more than
two days together without writing to you. I have
often heard that fear makes people loving.

MEN (*Sound gavel*): Adjourned. Till September.

(THEY *remove the desk, chairs, lecterns;* JOHN
argues with them.)

JOHN: I could not vote for this! We ought to have had
in our hands a month ago the whole legislative,
executive, and judicial of the nation—and raised a
naval power—

(*The* GIRL *runs to the platform;* ABIGAIL *sits up.*)

ABIGAIL: Dearest friend—

JOHN: —we have a continental treasury to establish—

ABIGAIL: I must be the bearer of what will greatly afflict
you.

(SHE *comes down past the* GIRL.)

Your brother Elihu lies very dangerously sick, his
life is despaired of.
JOHN (*Turns*): Elihu?
ABIGAIL: Your mother is with him in great anguish. The
return of thee, my dear partner—

(THEY *meet, embrace, their hands hungry for* EACH
OTHER.)

—is a pleasure I cannot express, but—darkened by—
JOHN (*Whispers*): Elihu?
ABIGAIL: —the loss of your brother.

(*The* GROUP *sings a dirge, Billings' Funeral Anthem;*
THEY *gather in cortege as around a grave upstage,*
with JOHN, ABIGAIL, *the* CHILDREN.)

MEN, WOMEN:
      I heard a great voice from heaven
      Saying unto me,
      Write, From henceforth
      Write, From henceforth
      Blessed are the dead—

(JOHN *speaks across the grave to the audience; the*
MOURNERS *stand with bowed heads.*)

JOHN: I followed the body of my youngest brother to
     the grave. He had commanded a company of militia
     outside Boston, and there taken a dysentery, epi-
     demic in the camp, of which he died, leaving a
     young widow and three young children, greatly
     lamented by all who knew him.

     (*Softly.*)

     And by none more than by me, who knew the
     excellence of his heart.

     (ABIGAIL *comes to touch his arm, the* OTHERS
     come down to the audience.)

MEN, WOMEN:
     Dysentery
     Of which he died
     Now will find
     Many a bed:

     Pestilence,
     Keep it in mind.

     Liberty, yes:
     Hunger and plague
     Are the spectres who ride,
     The horse is blind,
     And at its head
     Death is the guide.

(*The* GROUP *separate;* JOHN *is seated on the platform with a legal tome.*)

JOHN (*Reads*): "Statutes of the Realm, 1554. An act
whereby certain offenses be made treasons."

(*Perhaps the shadow of a noose dominates the* MAP
behind him.

The BOY *runs in;* HE *and* JOHN *gaze at each other,
mute. The* BOY *then peers at the page.*

ABIGAIL, *with a saddle bag for* JOHN's *departure,
comes to join them.*)

Politics are a path among red hot ploughshares.
Who then would run about barefoot among them?
Yet somebody must.

(HE *kisses the* BOY, *rises.*)

I must study politics and war, that my sons may
have liberty to study mathematics and philosophy.
My sons ought to study mathematics and philosophy, geography, commerce, agriculture, in order
to give their children a right to study painting,
poetry, music—

(HE *comes to kiss* ABIGAIL; *it is a leavetaking, not
easy.*)

ABIGAIL (*Then*): Is there a dearer name than friend?
Think of it for me.

JOHN: As for myself, I want to wander in my meadows
with her who has all my heart.

(HE *slowly backs away;* ABIGAIL *turns as* MAN 1
shoos the BOY *off and sits, his back to her.*)

ABIGAIL (*Calls*): I have met with some very ill treat-
ment—

(JOHN *retires upstage, stands with his back to her;*
ABIGAIL *addresses him at a distance.*)

In this day of distress for our Boston friends,
George Trott and family removed to Braintree and
applied to me if I could not accommodate him
with the next house. I sent for your tenant Mr.
Hayden—

(SHE *stares at* MAN 1, *seated with his back obstinate
throughout;* ABIGAIL *plays between their two
backs.*)

—and handsomely asked him. Mr. Trott said he
would go in with him. I let him have the dairy
room and the lower room; I asked Mr. Hayden
to remove his things into the other part of the
house. He said I was turning him out of door—

MAN 1 (*With her*): Turning me out of door to oblige Boston folks!

ABIGAIL (*A pause*): —and if you was at home you would not, but was more of a gentleman. I as mildly as I could represented the distress of Mr. Trott, removed my dairy things, and said that Mr. Trott should go in; I once more requested the old man to move into the other part of the house. He positively tells me he will not and all the art of man shall not stir him. Says Mr. Trott shall not—

MAN 1 (*With her*): Trott shall not come in!

ABIGAIL: What distresses the Boston people are driven to! yet that obstinate wretch will not remove his few things into the other part of the house. I had hard work to suppress my temper. I must take Mr. Trott in with me, and all his family.

I now desire you to give me orders whether his things may be removed into the other part of the house whether he consents or not? I own I shall be much mortified if you do not support me. I told the old man I should be justified by you—

MAN 1: Cannonball!

ABIGAIL: —he says cannonball shall not move him! I feel too angry to make this anything further than a letter of business, I am most sincerely yours, Abigail Adams.

(ABIGAIL *marches up to join the* WOMEN. JOHN *now turns down, his bag in hand, and encounters* MAN 2.)

JOHN: Philadelphia. I met Mr. Dickinson on foot in
Chestnut Street—

(MAN 2 *passes haughtily by*; JOHN *stares*.)

We are not to be on—speaking terms?

(MAN 1 and WOMAN 1 *walk past*; JOHN *bows*, THEY
too snub him.)

Or bowing terms—

(*The* OTHERS *circle past him, a frigid group*; SOME
*set the center platforms as two rooms back to
back*.)

MEN, WOMEN:
Freeze him out.

Listen to him
We'll live on air,
No trade, no law
Hack
The kingdom limb from limb—
JOHN (*To them*): The King has caught delegates as I
have often caught a horse, by holding out an empty
hat as if it was full of corn—
MEN, WOMEN:
Our hope

Is freeze him out.

This pepperpot
With the hot
Tongue, hear this, will serve
On ninety committees,
Chair
Some twenty-five, and preach
Revolution to each:

Is there a doubt
He'll burn the cities
Bare?

JOHN: We shall have to resist by force—

MEN, WOMEN:

Listen to him
We'll walk on air
From a rope.

(JOHN *watches them retire;* THEY *pass* ABIGAIL, *who comes opening a letter.*)

JOHN: Independence is a hobgoblin so frightful it throws delicate persons into fits to look it in the face.

ABIGAIL (*Reading*): "I saw this profound and enlightened patriot walk our streets alone, an object of nearly universal detestation—"

JOHN (*Glum*): Don't imagine from all this that I am in the dumps. Far otherwise.

(ABIGAIL *gazes upon him;* HE *tries to make light of it.*)

All great changes are irksome to the human mind. We must allow for a great deal of the ridiculous, much of the melancholy—

(HE *starts away from her, turns back.*)

—and some of the marvelous.

(HE *mounts the platform as to his room, opens his bag, digs out papers, including his notebook.*)

ABIGAIL: Tomorrow will be three weeks since you left. You may remember our farmboy Isaac was unwell. A violent dysentery was the consequence—

JOHN (*Jots in notebook*): One thing for my wife, who will be peeping here.

ABIGAIL: Two days after, I was seized with the same disorder.

JOHN: An English gentleman was with us, a man of penetration—

ABIGAIL: Our little Tommy was the next, and he lies very ill now—

(SHE *goes up, where in dim light the* GROUP *begin to gather in a sickbed scene.*)

JOHN: —and this penetrating gentleman thought Mrs. Adams the most accomplished lady he had seen since he came out of England.

(*To her, teasing*):

Down, vanity—

ABIGAIL (*Unhearing*): Yesterday cousin Patty was seized, and took a puke. Mr. Trott and one of his children are taken with the disorder. Our house is a hospital in every part.

(MAN 1 *sounds the gavel.* JOHN *gathers papers, starts down;* MAN 3 *sets the desk for him.*)

Mrs. Randall has one child that is not expected to live out the night. Deacon Adams has lost one.

(MAN 3 *gives* JOHN *a letter.*)

JOHN: I have not received one scratch of a pen from anybody till—

(HE *frowns reading.*)

ABIGAIL: Cousin Patty is very bad. Dr. Tufts tells me he has between sixty and seventy patients now sick with this disorder.

JOHN (*Turns*): The ill usage you received from Hayden I will not endure. I send a warning to him to go

out of the house immediately; let two or three wit-
nesses see it.

(MAN 3 *brings chair*; JOHN *sits*; THEY *confer over
papers.* ABIGAIL *comes halfway down to them.*)

ABIGAIL: So sickly and so mortal a time the oldest man
does not remember; my letter will be only a bill of
mortality.

JOHN (*Mutters*): Sundry letters from London—

(*The* WOMEN *upstage commence to pray, in
whispers.*)

ABIGAIL: Mrs. Randall has lost her daughter, Mrs.
Bracket hers. I know of eight this week who have
been buried in this town; eighteen have been buried
in the other parish since you left us, three and four
funerals in a day for many days.

JOHN (*Rises*): A motion! That a committee prepare a
plan for intercepting two British vessels which are
on their way with arms and powder.

ABIGAIL: Patty is bad, we cannot keep anything down
that she takes. Two of the children, John and
Charles, I have sent out of the house, to—

MAN 2 (*Down right*): It is the maddest idea in the
world to think of building an American fleet!

ABIGAIL (*Still trying for his ear*): —to keep them out
of the chamber—

MAN 1 (*Down left*): The most visionary mad project
    ever imagined!

JOHN: Talk of coping with Great Britain at sea would
    be quixotism, but—

MAN 2: An infant taking a mad bull by his horns—

JOHN: The question with me is can we defend our
    harbors and rivers. If we can, we can trade!

ABIGAIL: So much illness has occasioned a scarcity of
    medicines—

(JOHN *walks past* ABIGAIL *to argue from the map*.)

JOHN: My time has been spent upon the sea coast,
    attending courts at Plymouth, Barnstable, Martha's
    Vineyard; I have a confident opinion of our seamen.
    If they are let loose upon the ocean they will begin
    naval operations to the relief of our wants, as well
    as to the distress of the enemy.

ABIGAIL (*At platform*): I sit down with a heavy heart, I
    have had no other since you left me. Sister Elihu
    Adams lost her youngest child last night with this
    disorder.

(MAN 3 *confers with* MAN 1.)

Thus does pestilence travel in the rear of war. I
    think I shall never be wedded to the world, so un-
    certain are all its enjoyments—

JOHN (*Notices her*): My dear, the post brought me a

line from Mrs. Warren that you had been a little
unwell, but was much better.

(HE *scans the* MAP *before coming down to her*.)

I want to be informed from hour to hour of Boston,
and everything which passes in our army.

ABIGAIL: We live in daily expectation that Cousin
Patty will not continue many hours. A general
putrefaction seems to have taken place—

(JOHN *rejoins* MAN 1 *&* 3; THEY *concur, nod*.)

We cannot bear the house, we are constantly
cleansing it with hot vinegar.

(SHE *rises, joins the scouring* WOMEN.)

MAN 1: Be it resolved—

JOHN (*At desk, a motion*): —that Washington apply to
the Massachusetts for two armed vessels to inter-
cept the two British brigs—

MAN 3: —both the armed vessels of Rhode Island—

MAN 1: —the largest vessel in Connecticut—

JOHN: —and that the said vessels of war be on the
continental risk and pay.

(THEY *wait*; ABIGAIL *turns*.)

ABIGAIL: Dearest friend, woe follows woe—

(MAN 1 *sounds gavel.*)

MAN 3: Resolved!

ABIGAIL: My dear mother has taken the disorder, and is possessed by the idea that she shall not recover—

(SHE *comes to them, but* JOHN *and the* TWO MEN *walk upstage;* ABIGAIL *stares at the empty desk.*)

I never found the communication so difficult; tis only in my night visions that I know anything about you.

JOHN (*To* MEN): The proceedings of this day constitute the true origin of an American navy—

ABIGAIL: Tis allotted me to go to the sick and almost dying bed of my mother, and stay twelve hours with her, and then return home to cousin Patty, who—

(SHE *walks a step or two back to the* WOMEN, *stands averted.*)

—is now become so putrid a mass as scarcely to be able for anyone to do their duty towards her.

JOHN (*To* MEN): We must bend our attention to gunpowder. We must make it, I am determined never to have it out of my mind, it must be had.

(*The* MEN *retire;* JOHN *contemplates the* MAP.

ABIGAIL *slowly turns, speaks across to the empty desk.*)

ABIGAIL: I have just returned from attending Patty to the grave. She has lain five weeks, the most ghastly object my eyes ever beheld, so loathsome and pitiable. She made the fourth corpse that was this day committed to the ground.

(*The* WOMEN *keen.*)

How long O Lord, shall the whole land say I am sick?

JOHN: My dear, I have found great want of the art of copying plans, especially of America. I entreat you to teach this to my little girl and boys. It is as pretty an amusement as dancing.

(HE *comes back to the desk, picks up letters, sits to read.*

ABIGAIL *falls to her knees.*)

ABIGAIL: Have pity upon me, have pity upon me, O thou my beloved! for the hand of God presseth me sore. Yet will I not open my mouth because thou, O Lord, hast done it.

How can I tell you (O my bursting heart) that my dear mother has left me, this day about five o'clock she left this world.

Blessed spirit, where are thou?

JOHN (*Worried*): I received your two letters. I hope
that Patty is upon the recovery. I never had the
least intimation that any of my family was ill—

ABIGAIL: At times I am ready to faint under this stroke,
separated from thee who used to be a comforter
towards me.

JOHN: I thought of setting off immediately for Braintree. Yet the state of public affairs—

(MAN 2 *sounds gavel.*)

—debates—

MAN 2 (*Offering it*): A contract with Willing & Mor-
ris—

(JOHN *hits the desk, rises;* MAN 2 *is ironically
deferential.*)

For gunpowder—

JOHN: By which they will make a clear profit of twelve
thousand pounds without any risk at all! Such a
rage for profit, I sometimes think that although
we are engaged in the best cause that ever yet
employed the human heart, success is doubtful.

(MAN 3 *brings* JOHN *a letter, retires.*)

Liberty can no more exist without virtue than the
body can live without a soul—

(HE *breaks off, reads to himself.*)

ABIGAIL: You will forgive my wanderings of mind, I
cannot be correct—

(SHE *mounts the platform.*)

JOHN: "Dear sir, since your absence your family has
been visited with such a scene of sickness as it
never before saw. Mrs. Adams I pity under the—"

(HE *sits, shaken.*)

"—loss of her mother, at whose funeral she was
yesterday—"

(ABIGAIL *above sits on her bed, fingering a black
veil:* JOHN *is motionless over the letter, below.*
OTHERS *now, on their knees in half-light, scattered,
heads bowed, suggest the dead in a graveyard.*)

ABIGAIL: I have not been composed enough to write you
since last Sabbath, when in the bitterness of my
soul I wrote a few confused lines. That morning I
went into my mother's room with a cup of tea in
my hand, raised her head to give it to her, she swal-
lowed a few drops, gasped, and fell back upon her
pillow, opened her eyes with a look that pierced my
heart; it was the eagerness of a last look, which I
shall never forget.

It makes my heart ache to see my father. He said to me the other day, Child, I see your mother, go to what part of the house I will.

(JOHN *stands, faces her*; SHE *is bitter.*)

Lord, show us wherefore it is that thou art thus contending with us? In a very particular manner I have occasion to make this inquiry who have had breach upon breach, nor has one wound been permitted to be healed ere it is made to bleed afresh, in six weeks I count five of my near connections laid in the grave.

(JOHN *comes near her.*)

Your aunt died at Milton about ten days ago with the dysentery.

JOHN (*Softly*): My best friend.

It is the constitution under which we are born that if we live long ourselves we must bury our parents and many who are younger. I have lost a parent, a child, and a brother, to the house appointed for all flesh; our lives are not in our own power.

ABIGAIL: Yea, though he slay me I will trust in him, said holy Job.

JOHN: I bewail the loss of your mother—for nobody more than my children; her example, I have ever relied upon in my own mind for the education

of these little swarms. My children are the better
for the hand of their grandmother.

Whatever is preparing for us, let us receive. We
have no security against calamities here, this planet
is its region.

(The lights begin to fade, the GROUP OF DEAD *hum
like a wind rising, the percussion makes icy sounds.*

The MAP *enlarges to show what is now spoken of:
Boston still ringed, Braintree below it; the crawling
progress of cannon from Ticonderoga to Boston;
the American attack upon and retreat from
Quebec.)*

MEN, WOMEN:
        Dead
        In the sleet and ice
        Of bitter places
        That bitter December:

        (Three speakers, as indented.)

        Braintree, yes
                and who will remember
                Ticonderoga, the cannon I cursed
                and dragged on my ass over mountains
                        and who will remember
                        Quebec, where I fought
                        and why?

      eighty cannon on sleds
      and
           the bastards are headed south
           some bastard said
           and
   who will remember
      sinking in rivers and
      farmlands in sleet for forty days
      and
           the last thing I saw
      down to the sea
           the ice was red
           at my mouth,
           and
      the cannon to blow Boston free
      was there but
   our faces
           who will remember

None,
When the war is won
And the weather washes our stains
Out of the places,
And nothing of us remains but

Liberty, yes,
That star-spangled slut in every orator's bed,
Had by all.

Except the dead.

(JOHN *sits on his bed;* HE *and* ABIGAIL *are back to back.*)

JOHN: I think, if ever I come here again, I must bring you with me.

ABIGAIL: Hayden does not stir. Says he will not go out unless he is carried out.

JOHN: The most agreeable time I spend here is writing to you, and conversing with you when I am alone. I hope to be with you at Christmas—

ABIGAIL: Tis almost twelve o'clock at night. Adieu. I will only ask you to measure by your own the affection of your dearest friend—

(*The lights on her fade.*)

JOHN: —and be excused from coming here again. But I will never come here again without you.

(*The lights on him fade.*

The actors remain in position until the house lights are up, then leave the stage.)

ACT II

House lights down; stage empty.

The MAP *shows, as before, the crawling line of cannon from Ticonderoga to Boston, besieged, the British within.*

The kettledrum rumbles; a roar of cannon mounts. ABIGAIL, *the* WOMEN, CHILDREN *run in and downstage, to stare out.*

ABIGAIL: Tis a cannonade from *our* army!

(JOHN *and* MAN 3 *run in, opposite;* ABIGAIL *calls to him.*)

I have just returned from the hill, I could see every shell which was thrown. The rattling of the windows, the jar of the house, the continental roar of twenty-four pounders—Some very important crisis seems at hand—

(*Abrupt silence.*)

The ships are all drawn round the town, and movements amongst the British as if they meant to—

(*On the* MAP, *a British arrow puts out to sea from Boston.*)

—to leave Boston!
Bunker Hill is abandoned and every British soldier decamped this morning on board the transports! From our hill we have a view of the largest fleet ever seen in America, upwards of one hundred and seventy sail, they look like a forest!

JOHN: I give you joy of Boston, once more the habitation of Americans!

(*The* MEN *gather in a buzz,* JOHN *with them; the joyful* WOMEN *congregate with* ABIGAIL, SHE *speaks to them.*)

ABIGAIL: Every foot of ground which they obtain now they must fight for, and may they at a Bunker Hill price!

JOHN: The expectation here is that our enemies will be at Virginia.

(HE *studies the* MAP, *points.*)

New York will be their object.

(MAN 3 *joins him at the* MAP; ABIGAIL *to the* WOMEN.)

ABIGAIL (*Small talk*): Do not you want to see Boston? I am fearful of the smallpox or I should have been in.

JOHN: We shall have hot work in war.

ABIGAIL: A month ago we knew not whether we could plant with safety; now we sit under our own vine and—

JOHN: Make us acquainted with everything that is wanted—men, money, arms, tents, forage—

(MAN 3 *starts out;* JOHN *calls after him.*)

—and the state of the smallpox. It is the king of terrors.

ABIGAIL: I feel a gaiety de coeur to which before I was a stranger—

(SHE *and the* WOMEN *retire.*

The lights begin to dim; JOHN *is alone in the hall, lights a candle, comes back with it.*)

JOHN: The most dangerous part is to glide from under the old government into a *contented* submission to new. Is the subject too dry? To me, no romance is more entertaining.

(HE *sets the candle down, sits in the chair with paper, begins to write; it is now night on stage.*)

"Thoughts on Government."

(*On the step to her room* ABIGAIL *reappears, gazes toward him as* HE *mulls.*)

Kings have done much wrong, but the mob not less—

ABIGAIL: Oh, that I could annihilate space—

(SHE *does, walks over, and sitting on a platform near him, chin in hand, drinks him in.*)

JOHN (*Writing*): Allow the truth that all men are ferocious monsters when their passions are unrestrained; they murder like weasels for the pleasure of murdering.
Prepare bridles for them.

ABIGAIL: I long to hear that you have declared an independency—and in the new code of laws I desire you would remember the ladies.

JOHN (*Writing*): A legislative, an executive, and a judicial power comprehend the whole of government.

ABIGAIL: Be more generous than your ancestors, do not put such power into the hands of the husbands.

JOHN (*Writing*): It is by—balancing each of these powers against the other two that the tyranny in human nature can alone be checked. Arm a power above it and below it, both able to say when it grows mad, "Maniac! keep within your limits."

ABIGAIL: That your sex is naturally tyrannical admits of no dispute, but if attention is not paid to the ladies we are determined to foment a rebellion, and will not hold ourselves bound by any laws in which we have no representation.

JOHN: The principal difficulty lies in a representative assembly. It should be in miniature an exact portrait of the people at large—

(HE *writes on by candlelight;* ABIGAIL *gazes about.*)

ABIGAIL: A quiet night, no alarms, no cannon—

(SHE *rises, turns to contemplate him as* HE *writes, oblivious to her.*)

Nabby is sick with the mumps.

(HE *writes on,* SHE *waits.*)

Johnny has the mumps.

(HE *writes on,* SHE *waits.*)

Charles has the mumps.

(HE *writes on.* SHE *paces away, restless.*)

What can be the reason I have not heard from
you? My nights are tortured, I fear you are sick—

(*A knot of* WOMEN *in the shadows up right awaits
her; drawn to them,* SHE *glances back.*)

Write me, write me—it is my food by day and my
rest by night—

(SHE *joins the* WOMEN. JOHN *snuffs out the candles;
full lights up;* HE *rubs his eyes.*)

OHN: My dear, I concluded to borrow a little time from
my sleep and have written ten sheets about government; what will come of this, time will discover.

(OTHER DELEGATES *enter with portfolios;* JOHN
rises.)

Put under types, it goes to North Carolina—

(HE *seeks out each* DELEGATE *passing to present a
sheet.*)

—New Jersey—Virginia—

(*The* DELEGATES *scan the sheets, walk, stop, discuss
them sotto voce.*)

—other provinces.

(HE *turns to* ABIGAIL *and the* WOMEN, *earnest in conversation.*)

As to your code of laws—we are told that our struggle loosens the bands everywhere, children are disobedient, colleges turbulent, Negroes insolent; but yours is the first intimation that another tribe are discontented—

ABIGAIL (*Over her shoulder*): Several in town have broke out with the smallpox. If it should spread, only one thing—

(MAN 3 *sounds the gavel.*)

JOHN (*Eager*): Debates—

(HE *hurries back to take part;* ABIGAIL *calls.*)

ABIGAIL: —only one thing will prevent my going to Boston to be inoculated with our children, I—

MAN 3: Resolutions! concerning—

MAN 1: Indian Affairs.

MAN 2: Revenue matters.

ABIGAIL: I should run you in debt—

MAN 1: Naval arrangements—

JOHN (*Objecting.*) Twenty things are thrown in the way of the great subject, independence—

MAN 2: Coins and currencies.

MAN 1: Sundry petitions for—

JOHN: The time is consumed on trifles! I was ripe for
    explicit declarations twelve months ago—
MAN 2: Agriculture.
MAN 1: Port regulations.

(MAN 3 sounds the gavel. THEY *disperse*; JOHN
catches MAN 2 *by the elbow.*)

JOHN: The little pamphlet was for the sake of inviting
    your attention to the subject—

(HE *stops* MAN 1 *passing.*)

Come with the voice of Maryland—

MAN 3 (*Joins him*): —in favor of independence—
JOHN (*Back to* MAN 2): It must come—nibble and
    piddle and dribble, waste time, treasure, blood—
    we must come to it at last!

(THEY *are gone*; JOHN *stares off*, ABIGAIL *behind
him.*)

ABIGAIL: I should run you in debt for it.

(JOHN *hears, does not turn.*)

You promised to come see me in May.

(HE *shuts her voice out of his ears.*)

Or June.

JOHN: Journeys of such a length are expensive of time
and money, neither of which are my own—

ABIGAIL (*In dismay*): Do you determine to stay out
the year?

JOHN: I live a life of a man in a barrel spiked with
nails!

(HE *turns, avoiding her, crosses back toward the
chair.*)

ABIGAIL: Can you tell how I feel when the—youngest
come to me with a Ma—

(SHE *is pointing at the group of* WOMEN *where the*
GIRL, *unseen, is heard.*)

GIRL: Ma, when will Pa come home?

(JOHN *wheels, flaring.*)

JOHN: Every colony must institute a government! All
must be confederated together in a solemn contract! They must be declared free and independent
states! These things once finished, I shall think I
have answered the end of my creation—

ABIGAIL: The idea of a year—dissolves all my philosophy—

(*A silence.*)

JOHN (*Low*): We have lost a delegate to the smallpox. He would not be inoculated, he must take it in the natural way and die. Run me in debt.

(*After a long moment* ABIGAIL *turns, joins the* WOMEN; THEY *shift her platform.*

JOHN *turns to the* MAP, *which now shows the British arrow at sea curving from Boston down to New York; an American arrow points down overland. One by one, the* OTHERS *come around him to study it;* MAN 2 *is the questioner, urgent.*)

MEN, WOMEN:
New York *is* their object—

Staten Island their base,
And the bay
Brimful of their fleet—

No word?

Washington
Marching from Boston, I heard,
A race—

No word
Of peace?

Washington

Into Manhattan, I heard,
Hurrying men into place—

Dismay
In the town—

No word
Of peace
From the crown?

(MAN 3 *sounds the gavel;* HE *has a document.*)

MAN 3: From London. The American Prohibitory Act of
Parliament—

(JOHN *and the* OTHERS *are at him in a circle to
read it.* ABIGAIL *has settled the* CHILDREN *into reclin-
ing positions upstage of the moved platform;* SHE
sits, overseeing them.)

ABIGAIL: I now date from Boston, where I yesterday
arrived and was with all four of our little ones inoculated for the smallpox. The paper currency has
spread it everywhere.

(*The* GROUP *commences a mutter which will
crescendo throughout;* JOHN *breaks out of it.*)

JOHN: In spite of all our supplications!

(HE *steps toward* ABIGAIL *in excitement.*)

The Prohibitory Act of Parliament throws thirteen
colonies out of the royal protection! This act *makes*
us independent—

ABIGAIL: The children are not yet broke out. I dread it
more than before I saw it—

(*Back,* JOHN *argues with the circle, pointing at
the* MAP.)

JOHN: We cannot command the resources of our own
country, cannon, powder, ships, without the powers
of government—

ABIGAIL (*Racked*): A most—excruciating pain in my
head, and every limb—

(*The mutter rises in the circle;* JOHN *hurries to*
ABIGAIL, *who breathes more easily.*)

JOHN: I hang upon tenterhooks, I have not yet learned
how you fare—

ABIGAIL: —now free from pain. All my sufferings produced but one eruption.

JOHN: I find through all the colonies plans resembling
that in "Thoughts on Government"—the colonies
are turning their eyes that way—

ABIGAIL: Charles has not had one symptom. Johnny has
it exactly as one would wish, he is cleverly.

JOHN (*To the circle*): The question is a declaration in
words!

(*To her.*)

You cannot make thirteen clocks strike precisely
alike at the same second—
ABIGAIL: Nabby's eruption was trifling.

(MAN 3 *hurries out of the circle*; JOHN *meets him.*)

MAN 3: Committees from every county vote Pennsyl-
vania—
JOHN: Pennsylvania for independence!
ABIGAIL: Tommy has a dozen out, and is very gay.
MAN 3: New York acts in character—
JOHN: There is neither spunk nor gumption in that
province—
ABIGAIL (*Worried*): What to do with Charley I know
not; I cannot get the smallpox to operate upon
him. I have had inoculation repeated.
JOHN (*To her*): Every post and every day rolls in upon
us Independence like a torrent—
MAN 3: Georgia, Virginia—
JOHN (*Pointing*): Four to the southward agreed with
four to the northward, five in the middle not so
ripe—
MAN 3: Maryland—
JOHN: Maryland I have often wished would exchange
places with Halifax!

ABIGAIL: I receive your letters—a fine parcel, a feast to
    me—
JOHN (*To her*): I feel like a savage to be here, but I
    cannot leave. Business—

   (MAN 1 *sounds the gavel; the circle disperses,*
   WOMEN *to sides,* MEN *into session.*)

MAN 3: Resolutions concerning independency!
JOHN: —which must not stop for anything—

   (HE *hurries back;* ABIGAIL *handles the letters.*)

MAN 1 (*Sounds gavel*): Referred till tomorrow morning.
JOHN (*A motion*): Resolved! that—
MAN 2 (*Sounds gavel*): Referred to the whole Congress.
JOHN: —that no time be lost, a—
MAN 1 (*Sounds gavel*): Postponed to the first of July.
JOHN: —a committee to prepare a declaration—
MAN 2 (*Sounds gavel*): Ordered to lie on the table.
JOHN (*Furious*): I don't know whether Job should be
    reckoned the patient man, it seems to me I have
    had more trials than he!

   (HE *marches fuming up center to sit at the back;*
   the other MEN *adjourn, joining the* WOMEN *here*
   and there; ABIGAIL *shows the letters to the* CHIL-
   DREN.)

ABIGAIL: I am really astonished at the number.

(SHE *unfolds one, reads to them.*)

"July first, 1776. This morning is assigned for the greatest debate of all—"

(*A hush now, no movement,* ALL *standing in place:* JOHN *is very attentive, and behind him the* MAP *shows two military fronts:* (1) *an American line at Ticonderoga with a British arrow threatening from Quebec;* (2) *an American line at New York with a British arrow in the bay.*)

MEN, WOMEN:
    Retreat
    Was the cry in the gales
    Of Quebec; at Ticonderoga this day
    Riflemen
    Half dead of smallpox
    Lie,
    Make bullets of nails,
    And wait
    For the thickets to shrill
    With invasion—

    New York, the fleet
    Stands off for the kill;
    Washington rides
    Along his lines, where gunners
    Eye
    The winds, and the tides,

And a growing thicket of sails
That fill
With invasion—

ABIGAIL (*Reading*): "—a greater question never will
be decided—"

JOHN (*A whisper*): Don't divide.

ABIGAIL: "Mr. Dickinson in a speech of great eloquence
combined all that had been said against it. No
member rose to answer him; and after waiting, in
hopes of someone less—obnoxious than myself—"

(*A wait;* JOHN *then rises slowly, and comes down
to us.*)

JOHN: Don't divide.
We are in the midst of a revolution, the most complete, unexpected, and remarkable in the history of
nations. If ever a war could be called the people's
war, it is this, determined on by the people and
pursued by the people; the American cause stands
upon the character of the people. The war is only
a consequence; the revolution is in the minds of the
people. The decree has gone forth and cannot be
recalled, a more equal liberty than in other parts
of the earth must be established in America.
Let the choice be unanimous.
I am not without apprehensions. The people will
have unbounded power; and the people are ex-
tremely addicted to corruption and venality.

But on such a full sea are we now afloat that we must trust to winds and currents, with the best skill we have. You and I have been sent into life at a time when the greatest lawgivers of antiquity would have wished to live. When before had three millions of people power and opportunity to establish the happiest government that human wisdom can contrive?

Don't divide.

I am well aware of the toil and blood and treasure that it will cost us to maintain this Declaration. Yet through all the gloom I see the rays of ravishing light; posterity will triumph in this day's transaction. Objects of the most stupendous magnitude, and the lives and liberties of millions yet unborn, are before us.

Don't divide. Let the choice be unanimous, I beg—

(HE *waits in appeal, unmoving. Then* ABIGAIL *rises, half mounts the center platform, facing off; the* GROUP *is now hers.*)

ABIGAIL: I went with the multitude into King Street to hear the proclamation for independence read from the balcony of the State House.

MAN 1 (*Unseen*): "We hold these truths to be self-evident, that all men are created equal—"

ABIGAIL (*Turns*): The King's arms were taken down, and every vestige of him burnt. Thus ends royal authority, and all the people shall say, Amen.

(*Now the* GROUP *breaks loose—"Amen! Amen!"—
and rips down the royal flag in Congress, and retires
pell-mell to the rear;* ABIGAIL *returns to her* CHIL-
DREN.)

I have not got rid of my terrors of the smallpox—
JOHN: My dear, I would joyfully agree to the smallpox
    for the sake of the company. I am now determined
    to go home.

(*Now* HE *moves to mount the platform as his
room;* HE *sits to write.*)

ABIGAIL (*With the* BOY): Charles has taken it in the
    natural way!
JOHN (*In exhaustion*): To the Massachusetts. The
    necessity of fresh delegates.
ABIGAIL: He has above a thousand pussels as large as a
    great green pea—
JOHN: Sam Adams is completely worn out, his strength
    and spirit exhausted; my own case worse—
ABIGAIL (*To him*): Charles has taken it in the *natural*
    way!
JOHN (*Hears, is stricken*): Charley—my dear Charley?—
ABIGAIL (*Back*): —a stupefaction and delirium—
JOHN: —symptoms so terrible—indicate the utmost
    danger—
ABIGAIL (*Overlapping*): Where I entertained one terror
    before, I do ten now—

JOHN: I did not know what fast hold that little prattler had upon me—

ABIGAIL (*A wail*): I think I have all my difficulties to grapple with, separate from my earthly prop and support—

JOHN (*To her*): Ask the General Court if they can send me horses; if they cannot, send them yourself.

(MAN 3 *mounts to his room with a paper*; JOHN *whirls on him.*)

Go home I will if I leave the Massachusetts without a member here! I will give any man a pension out of my own private funds to take my place! *Somebody—you—must—send!*

(*A silence.* ABIGAIL *then settles beside the* BOY, *half in tears.*)

ABIGAIL: Charley is better. We think he will do well.

(JOHN *is rigid, listening.*)

I was talking of horses for you when little Charles who lay upon a couch covered over with smallpox, and nobody knew he heard, lifted up his head and says—

BOY (*A whisper*): Mama, take my dollar and get a horse for Papa.

(JOHN *sits, holds his head, is hoarse.*)

JOHN: I wish to be relieved from Philadelphia forever.

ABIGAIL: This is a beautiful morning. I came here with all my treasure of children, have passed through a most terrible disease, and not one of us is wanting.

MAN 3: From General Washington—

(JOHN *scans the paper; the sounds of war rise.*)

The decision of a Council of War—

JOHN: —*for quitting Long Island?*

(HE *stares,* MAN 3 *nods;* JOHN *points to him to sit and write.*)

ABIGAIL: I have spent three days almost entirely with you, reading over the letters I have, and thinking of my friend—

JOHN (*Grim*): To General Parsons.

ABIGAIL: —my absent friend—anticipating a meeting, my heart would palpitate with the idea—

JOHN (*Dictating, harsh*): There was a flight from Quebec; I fear retreat from New York; we shall perish in infancy.

(*Savagely.*)

Our officers were not acquainted with the ground; they had never reconnoitered the enemy; they had

neither spies, sentries, nor guards placed as they
ought to have been. Ancient generals have been
nailed to gibbets alive for such crimes!

ABIGAIL: —and I have held you to my bosom till my
whole soul has dissolved in tenderness, and my
pen fallen from my hand—

(MAN 3 *hurries out with the message.*)

JOHN (*A pause*): My dear, our affairs having taken a
turn at Long Island so much to our disadvantage—

ABIGAIL: I must write in another strain. My father sends
his horse, and Dr. Tufts another—they will set off
now—

JOHN (*With an effort*): —I cannot see my way clear
to return home as I intended.

(ABIGAIL *hears, is stricken.*)

Tell posterity one truth for me—

(*Gritty.*)

—and that is that I love my wife, and I have left
her to serve my country where I don't find anybody
I like so well.

(ABIGAIL *bows her head.*)

ABIGAIL: Shall I say, remember me?

JOHN (*It is almost a curse*): Posterity! You will never know how much your freedom cost the present generation; make good use of it. If not, I shall repent it in heaven that I ever took—half the pains—

(*The sounds of war rise.*

JOHN *returns to work among a scatter of papers in his room.*

OTHERS *enter and restore* ABIGAIL's *platform; the* GROUP *sit here and there to sing a forlorn ballad of the period.*)

MEN, WOMEN:
There I sat on Buttermilk Hill,
Who could blame me, cry my fill,
And every tear would turn a mill:
Johnny has gone for a soldier.

(ABIGAIL *paces in solitude.*)

Me oh my, I loved him so,
Broke my heart to see him go,
And only time will heal my woe:
Johnny has gone for a soldier.

(ABIGAIL *goes up to her room, next to* JOHN'S; SHE *has a basket of old letters which* SHE *commences to go through.*)

ABIGAIL: 1763.

(SHE *reads excerpts aloud,* JOHN *at first not hearing.*)

To Abigail Smith, Weymouth. "I mount this morning for that noisy town of Boston, where pomp, frippery, foppery, politics, and the wrangles of the law will give me the higher relish for next Sunday—"

(SHE *takes up another.*)

To John Adams, Braintree. "Have you heard the news? An apparition was seen one evening this week hovering about this house, which very much resembled you—"

(JOHN's *head comes up.*)

"How it should ever enter into the head of an apparition to assume a form like yours, I cannot devise."

(SHE *takes up another.*)

"Miss Adorable. I hereby order you—"

(JOHN *picks up on the text, slowly, remembering.*)

JOHN: "—to give as many kisses and as many hours of your company after nine o'clock as I please. Charge them to my account."

ABIGAIL (*Another*): "My friend. Here am I all alone in my chamber, a mere nun; after professing myself thus, it will not be out of character to confess, my thoughts are—often—"

(SHE *thinks better of continuing aloud;* SHE *looks at another.*)

"My dear—"

JOHN (*Simultaneously*): "My dear, learn to conquer your appetites. The conquest of the rebellious principles in our natures requires greater parts than the management of kingdoms. Did you ever read Epictetus?"

ABIGAIL (*Simultaneously, very dry*): "Did you ever read Epictetus?"

JOHN: "I am determined very soon to write you the main faults I have observed in you."

ABIGAIL (*Another*): "Heigh day, Mister what's your name, who taught you to threaten so vehemently? Why, my good man, tell me all my faults, be to me a second conscience."

(SHE *looks at another;* JOHN *stands, walks in his room.*)

JOHN: "In the first place, you have been negligent in attending so little to cards. Another is a certain modesty; you often hang your head like a bulrush—"

(HE *sits away from but facing her, gazing at her.*)

"—and the company loses the bright sparkles of those eyes. Another fault is still more inexcusable in a lady, I mean a habit of reading, writing, and thinking. Another is sitting with the legs across—"

(ABIGAIL *uncrosses her legs, takes another.*)

ABIGAIL: "I read over my faults with as much pleasure as another would their perfections. I think that a gentleman has no business to concern himself about the legs of a lady."

(SHE *takes another;* JOHN *watches her steadily.*)

JOHN: "Dear Madam. Steel and the magnet will not fly together with more celerity than somebody and somebody when brought within the striking distance—"

(ABIGAIL *reads another slower.*)

ABIGAIL: "My dearest friend. My things will be ready, and then, sir, if you please you may take me. I

want not again to experience what I this morning
felt, when you left your—A. Smith."

(A *long silence between them*, ABIGAIL *bent over
the letters; then the sounds of war are audible
again*. DELEGATES *gather*, MAN 2 *sounds the gavel*.)

MAN 2: Established by Congress, a Board of War, J.
  Adams chairman, responsible for all armies and
  materiel.
JOHN (*To her*): It is absolutely necessary for a Congress
  to be sitting, and to have persons here not seized
  with an ague-fit.

(HE *rises, descends to the* DELEGATES; *the sounds of
war grow louder. The* WOMEN *and* CHILDREN *run
in below* ABIGAIL, *some to point at the* MAP, *which
shows the retreat now spoken of*.)

WOMEN:
    Driven back!

    Retreat
    Is the word, New York in flames,
    Hessians
    On the attack—
ABIGAIL (*Up*): Tis said they will take Hudson's River—
WOMEN:
    Fort Washington taken,
    With thousands of men—

ABIGAIL (*Anxious*): —can they cut off communications between the colonies?

(SHE *is half down among them, has the* CHILDREN *by the hand, is searching for* JOHN *among the delegates.*)

WOMEN:
Fort Lee is forsaken!

Again
Driven back,
South—

Through the Jerseys—

(*The sounds of war fade.*)

ABIGAIL: Tis said Washington has but eight thousand troops with him—
WOMEN:
Five thousand—

Four—

In retreat
To the Delaware—
ABIGAIL (*Dismayed*): Can it be true?
WOMEN:
Defeat

Is the word
In every mouth—

(THEY *turn away slowly, leaving;* ABIGAIL *stands, with the* GIRL.

JOHN *is seated with* MEN 1 *and* 3 *around the desk, making notes, a committee meeting over memos.* JOHN *is worn out, coughing, testy.*)

JOHN: Congress must assume a discipline over officers. The frequent surprises by which our officers are taken convince me there is a dearth of genius among them.

ABIGAIL (*To the* GIRL): May we learn from defeat—the power of becoming invincible—

(SHE *sits the* GIRL *to sew, steps outdoors to look out over the land.*)

MAN 3 (*With a memo*): J. Adams and T. Jefferson to revise the Articles of War—

JOHN: Whatever we report will be opposed, we might as well therefore report a complete system. Find out the name, character, behavior, and whole history of the brigadier generals and colonels—

ABIGAIL: This province has been drained for sea service as well as land; I hardly think you can be sensible of how much we are thinned.

JOHN: Make the most minute inquiry; I am determined
  to know that army and all its officers.
  (HE *takes up memos*; THEY *work in ledgers*):
  Powder.

ABIGAIL: If it is necessary, the women must reap the
  harvests.

JOHN: Casting for cannon.

ABIGAIL (*Back, to the* GIRL, *bright*): We wanted powder,
  we have a supply; we wanted guns, we have been
  favored; if our men are all drawn off and we are
  attacked—

JOHN: Paymaster funds.

ABIGAIL: —you will find Amazons in America; we will
  not be conquered.

  (SHE *kisses the* GIRL; THEY *smile, and both sew.
  The* BOY *comes in with letters.* JOHN *uncaps a bottle
  of medicine.*)

JOHN: Indians in the army.

ABIGAIL (*To him*): Master John has become post rider
  from Boston to Braintree. I received your letter—

JOHN: Canteens.

ABIGAIL (*Scanning it*): —and though I think it a choice
  one in the literary way, not one word respecting
  your health.

JOHN: Camp kettles.

ABIGAIL: I advised you to take for your cough rhubarb
  and calomel. Do not omit it. Take it immediately.

(HE *does. The* CHILDREN *kiss her, retire; alone, her mood lets down.*)

JOHN: Blankets.

ABIGAIL: I feel concerned lest your clothes should go to rags, having nobody to take care of you in—

(SHE *is lost in thought, depressed.*)
—your long absence—

JOHN: Tents.

ABIGAIL: I have a suit of homespun for you, whenever you—return—

(SHE *gathers it up, stands, gazes about.*)

JOHN: Shoes. Hose.

ABIGAIL: Unless you return, what little property you possess will be lost.

JOHN: Flints.

ABIGAIL: I do the best I can, it will not pay its way—

(SHE *goes upstairs, very lonely.*)

JOHN: Rations.

(*It is the last memo;* MEN 1 *and* 3 *close their ledgers.* JOHN *pushes his away, sits back in exhaustion.*)

The history of our Revolution will be one con-
tinued lie—that Franklin's electrical rod smote
the earth and out sprang General Washington—

(MEN 1 *and* 3 *remove their chairs, set up for a*
session; above, ABIGAIL *adds the letter to the*
basket.)

ABIGAIL: I never close my eyes at night till I have been
to Philadelphia—

(MAN 2 *sounds the gavel;* JOHN *rises with memos*
to speak.)

—and my first visit in the morning is there—
JOHN: The new army, the new army, there is no time to
be lost!

(*The* DELEGATES *confer;* HE *waits.* ABIGAIL *cannot*
shake off her mood; SHE *sits with the basket in*
her lap, staring.)

MAN 2 (*Sounds gavel*): Resolved! that eighty-eight
battalions be enlisted.

(*Adjourning, the* DELEGATES *retire;* JOHN *stands,*
too weary to move.)

JOHN: My dear, we have agreed upon forming a *regular*
army—to serve at last throughout the entire war—

(HE *drops the memos on the desk, leans on it a moment.*)

ABIGAIL: I have been told the communication would be cut off and you would not be ever able to return—

JOHN: I have been here until I am stupefied.

ABIGAIL: They tell me they heard you was dead—

JOHN: I suppose your ladyship has been in the twitters, but—

ABIGAIL (*It bursts out*): I *entreat* you to return!

JOHN: —I yesterday obtained leave of absence.

(*A pause. Then* SHE *rises;* JOHN *turns, slowly crosses to her;* SHE *is quick to be on the steps to receive him, but* THEY *both stop, gaze, stand untouching.*)

ABIGAIL: I need not tell you—every tender—

(THEY *are awkward with absence, physically shy;* ABIGAIL *half stammers.*)

There is one misfortune in our family which I never mentioned, it is—your grey horse. She lamed herself, a callus is grown upon her footlock joint. She was not with foal, as you imagined—

JOHN (*Touches her cheek, wry*): Keep her for the good she has done.

ABIGAIL: —but I hope she is now. Care has been taken in that—respect—

(HE *draws her into a deep kiss. Then* SHE *whispers.*)

Oh my dear friend, do you know how I feel when
I look back upon a long absence?

(THEY *turn upstairs, the lights dying on them;*
THEY *are lost to view in the silhouetted* GROUP,
which comes down around them.)

MEN, WOMEN:
 Man and wife,
 October, '76.

 Autumn
 No different then,
 Life
 Going underground, leaving
 The grass, and the standing corn;
 November,
 Rains, and the woodlands burning red
 Blown
 Barren as sticks;
 Burning low
 The cause and its campfires
 Hide
 In the hills back of the Delaware, grown
 Fanged with ice;
 December, and every creek
 Suspended,
 The landscape lifting its belly

Swollen with snow
Cries out, and the dead
Hand of winter writes on the eye
Like a thorn:

What
In this white and stricken bed of dying
Kicks
To be born?

(*The* GROUP *separates; lights grow on* JOHN *packing his bag upstairs,* ABIGAIL *helping, the* GIRL *waiting below.*)

JOHN (*Gloomy*): What shall I say to my children? What will they say to me, for leaving them so much to—the disposal of chance?
WOMAN 1:
    The disposal of chance—

(JOHN *comes downstairs to hug the* GIRL *to him; the* BOY *is upstairs when* JOHN *addresses* TOMMY, *and* JOHN QUINCY *and* CHARLES *are then seen in silhouette as grown,* MEN 1 *and* 2.)

JOHN: My dear daughter—
WOMAN 2:
    Romance
    Is her lot, she will marry
    Washington's aide.

JOHN: You write a handsome hand, now and then send a specimen of it to Philadelphia. I shall take pleasure in constant correspondence.

My dear Tommy, I believe I must change your title from General, and make a physician of you. To relieve your fellow creatures, is not this better than to be destroying mankind by thousands?

WOMAN 3:

Law

Will be his choice.

JOHN: John Quincy. When you grow up—

WOMAN 1:

Haunted

By a father's voice—

JOHN: —you will feel a curiosity to learn the history of the late Revolution; and if you should now and then meet with an incident which throws some light upon your father's character, I charge you to consider it with an attention only to truth.

WOMAN 1:

President

At his father's death.

JOHN: Charles, the delight of my eyes. You are a thoughtful child, you know, your sensibility exquisite: how are your feelings affected by the times? Before you are grown—

WOMAN 2:

Drunkard.

Sick, dirty,

Homeless—

JOHN: —I hope this war will be over—
WOMAN 2:
    Dead
    At thirty.
JOHN: May you enjoy the fruits of it.

> (HE *takes* ABIGAIL's *hands, searches her face; there is a special air between them.*)

I derive a secret pleasure from a—circumstance which I suppose occasions you apprehensions—
ABIGAIL: I want to hear from you every day.

> (JOHN *kisses her, and takes up the saddle bag, most reluctant.*)

JOHN: You will have patience with me this time, I hope, this time will be the last.

> (HE *goes up right with the bag; the* CHILREN *run a few steps after him and stop. A silence.*)

ABIGAIL (*Slowly*): I had it in my heart to dissuade him from going, and I know I could have prevailed—

> (*Her hand finds her belly.*)

—but our public affairs wore so gloomy an aspect—
WOMAN:
    '76.

Gone dark.
And what,
In this deathbed, kicks
To be born
Is—

(*Exploding sounds of gunfire spin the* MEN *coming
down with* JOHN *as delegates;* ABIGAIL *turns to
listen; the* MEN *are elated, shout, pummel each
other, point at the* MAP. *It shows the American attack on Trenton and Princeton, the British pullback
and Philadelphia in the clear.*)

MEN:

Trenton,
Trenton is won!
Over the Delaware deadly with ice and
Washington ah you
Boatfuls of men and horses and
Quiet as mice and
Over the Delaware skip like a ditch and
Smashing them twice and
The redcoats have run and
The Jerseys are free and
Washington ah you sonofabitch
Philadelphia is safe!

JOHN: My dear, our enemies divided their forces, two
thousands killed and taken. Oh, that the Continental Army was full!

ABIGAIL (*Pregnant*): I rejoice in our late successes.

(*The* WOMEN *bring the desk as a table and sit her to tea, a happy, ministering group.*)

JOHN (*To the* MEN): Be patient, time will bring forth, after the usual groans, a fine vigorous healthy boy—

(HE *bethinks himself, is amused, turns to* ABIGAIL *as the* MEN *scatter.*)

If it is a young lady, call her Elizabeth after your mother.

ABIGAIL: Tea, that baneful weed.

(MAN 3 *brings* JOHN *a report;* ABIGAIL *speaks to the* WOMEN.)

I think I have enjoyed as much health as I ever did in the like situation—

(MAN 3 *retires;* JOHN *takes the report up to his room, scrutinizes it.*)

—a situation I do not repine at, tis a constant remembrancer of an absent friend, and excites— sensations which are better felt than expressed.

(*The* WOMEN *laugh, rise, take their leave as* MEN 1 *and* 2 *come upstairs to* JOHN; HE *greets them with the report.*)

JOHN: The wrangles between officers! scrambling for rank and pay like apes for nuts.

(THEY *come in;* HE *gestures them where to sit, and digs other papers out;* ABIGAIL *is alone, toying with her cup.*)

ABIGAIL (*Softly*): I often sit myself down alone to think of you, tis a melancholy kind of amusement; whilst the weighty cares of state—

JOHN: Board of War reports—

(HE *gives them out, turns to* ABIGAIL *as the* MEN *study them.*)

ABIGAIL: —scarcely leave room for a sentiment to steal into the bosom of my friend.

JOHN: My dear, I have got into the old routine of War Office and Congress; from four o'clock in the morning till ten at night I have not a single moment which I can call my own—

ABIGAIL: I visit you almost every night, or you me, but waking—

JOHN: I hope my five or six babes are all well.

ABIGAIL: —waking, the agreeable delusion vanishes.

MAN 1 (*With report*): In the medical department—

JOHN (*Back*): We are making every regulation in our power.

MAN 1: The health of the men—

JOHN: —will be better provided for.

MAN 2: In the commissary's department—

JOHN (*Searching*): In the commissary's department—

ABIGAIL (*Wry*): We are told the most disagreeable
    things by use become less so. No separation was
    ever so painful to me.

JOHN (*Passing papers*): —large quantities of meat have
    been salted down. So that this department, which
    last year occasioned us such losses of men, is now
    in good order.

ABIGAIL: As to intelligence from Boston, every method
    is taking to fill up the Continental Army.

(SHE *is carrying the tea things off, but is stopped
    by something inaudible;* SHE *stands, listens.*)

JOHN: The armies begin to be respectable. We must
    not remit our exertions—

(Now HE *breaks off, to listen also; barely audible
    is a rhythmic ticking, which grows louder; the*
    OTHERS *run in, listen as the rhythm is added to by
    rustlings, animal calls, ship creakings.*)

MEN, WOMEN (*In whispers*):
    Indians.
    Transports.
    Hessians.
    And British.
    Burgoyne.

(*Sounds and* VOICES *mount in a crescendo*; SPEAKERS
refer to the MAP. *It shows the British arrow from
Quebec and Montreal down Lake Champlain,
aimed at Ticonderoga.*)

Setting sail.
From Canada.
Ten thousand.
South
By the lakes,
Burgoyne setting sail
For Ticonderoga,
The target is Ti,
The invasion
Breaks!

(THEY *scatter, run*; MAN 3 *is staring at the* MAP, *and*
JOHN *hastens to him*; MAN 2 *runs out.*)

JOHN (*Hot*): If Ticonderoga is lost, New England will
bear the blame. I have been abominably deceived
about our troops, not one New Englandman has
yet arrived.

(ABIGAIL *gathers the* CHILDREN, *her movements
heavier with pregnancy.*)

ABIGAIL: As the summer advances I have many anxieties
—some of which I should not feel if you could be
with me.

(MAN 3 *starts out but meets* MAN 2 *returning;* THEY *confer as* JOHN *and* MAN 1 *turn to the* MAP.)

JOHN: The Continental troops must all march to Ti. Ti is the place to stop the enemy.

(*The* CHILDREN *invert the table to play fort behind it,* ABIGAIL *watching.*)

ABIGAIL: I regret to wish away one of the most precious blessings of life, yet—

(*The* MAP *changes to show a British arrow thrusting out to sea from New York.*)

MAN 3 (*To John*):
    News
    We fear.

MAN 2:
    Howe and the fleet
    Have left New York,
    Target not known.

MAN 3:
    Boston.

MAN 2:
    Or here.

(*A silence; but* ABIGAIL *hears,* SHE *takes a step.*)

ABIGAIL (*On edge*): If you hear of our being invaded this way, I think you must return.

(JOHN *at last breaks the silence.*)

JOHN: If they come here they shall get little but bare walls.

(HE *claps one* MAN *on the arm, making it light.*)

We are too brittle ware to stand the dashing of balls and bombs—

ABIGAIL: I used to have courage, but—

(*The* MEN *separate;* JOHN *turns to* ABIGAIL, *still light.*)

JOHN: My dear, I hear nothing from you, but I am endeavoring to devise some better regulations of the post office. Don't be too much alarmed at an attack of Boston; Howe may attempt this town.

(HE *turns to the* MAP, *pondering;* ABIGAIL *sits on the platform step, somewhat relieved.*)

ABIGAIL: I confess I had rather he make a visit to you than to me at this time. I should make a miserable hand of running now. Master John says—

BOY (*From the fort*): Ma, I never saw anybody grow so fat as you do.

(JOHN *walks left, where* MAN 1 *hands him a raincoat and a few letters;* JOHN *glances through them.*)

ABIGAIL: Do you sigh for home? and would you share with me what I have to pass through? I could look pleasant upon you in the midst of—sufferings—

(*The* WOMEN *come, very quiet, shoo the* CHILDREN *away, are solicitous of* ABIGAIL; JOHN *hands the letters back.*)

JOHN (*To* MAN 1): I was never more desirous of hearing frequently from home—

ABIGAIL (*To* WOMEN): I do not expect it will be more than two weeks. I can but poorly walk about house.

(JOHN, *putting on the coat, speaks to* ABIGAIL *with the* WOMEN.)

JOHN: Will my brother Peter, when the time comes, officiate for me at a christening?

ABIGAIL (*Turns*): Mrs. Howard died yesterday. She was delivered of a daughter yesterday week, a mortification of her bowels occasioned her death. Everything of this kind naturally shocks a person in similar circumstances—

(SHE *begins upstairs, heavily, the lights fading, a sound of wind rising.* JOHN *turns up his collar.*)

JOHN: A long, cold, raw northeast storm has chilled our blood for two days. It is unusual. An omen, no doubt.

ABIGAIL (*Resting*): I sometimes imagine these separations as preparatory to a still more painful one—in which even hope, the anchor of the soul, is lost—

(*Lights down, except on* ABIGAIL'S *room as* SHE *lies down; the* WOMEN *and the* MEN *now stand scattered, their backs to us, motionless, heads bowed, suggestive again of a graveyard;* JOHN *walks among them.*)

JOHN: I spent an hour this evening in the congregation of the dead. I took a walk into the potter's field; the graves of the soldiers, upwards of two thousand during the last winter, are enough to make stone to melt.

ABIGAIL: I have been very unwell for this week past, with some complaints that are new to me—

JOHN (*Staring out*). Nothing from Howe and his banditti.

ABIGAIL: —I hope not dangerous.

(*The* WOMEN *move to gather below her; the* MEN *move into a muttering cluster, and* JOHN *joins them to listen.*)

The fruit was injured by the cold east winds, and falls off. Your—

(SHE *is shaken, gasps.*)

I must—bear what I cannot fly from—

JOHN (*To her*): —a confused account of something
    unlucky at Ticonderoga. I am much—afraid—
ABIGAIL: —and now I have endured it. I—

(WOMAN 1 *goes up to her;* JOHN *erupts out of the
cluster in anguish and rage.*)

JOHN: We have another Fort Washington affair at
    Ticonderoga!

(*The* MAP *shows the American retreat south.*)

I live here wasting my life, in labors to procure
cannon, ammunition, stores, clothing, for armies
who give them all away to the enemy without firing
a gun—
ABIGAIL (*To* WOMAN 1, *faint*): I was last night taken
    with a shaking fit, and am very apprehensive that
    a life was lost.

(WOMAN 2 *goes up to join them;* JOHN *storms back
to the* MEN.)

JOHN: I think we shall never defend a post until we
    shoot a general; after that we shall defend posts,
    and this event in my opinion is not far off!

(*The* MEN *stare at his half-lunatic rage, and edge
away;* WOMAN 3 *goes to* ABIGAIL.)

ABIGAIL (*Fainter*): I have no reason today to think otherways. What may be the consequences to me—

(SHE *makes an effort to speak past them to* JOHN.)

I can—add no more than that I am in every situation unfeignedly yours, yours—

(*The* WOMEN *gather round her, the lights die out on them.*

JOHN, *still in his coat, is left alone in half-light;* HE *sits in his chair, covers his face with a hand.*)

JOHN: I am weary of my employment, and almost of my life.

(*After a moment* HE *twists in the chair toward the obscure* WOMEN.)

My mind runs upon my family; I long to hear of the safety of my dearest friend. I had no letter by the last post—

(HE *rises, takes a few steps, stops.*)

But I ought not to be weary in endeavoring to do well.

(*In conflict, left or right,* HE *is drawn to and enters the house;* HE *haunts it like a ghost, searching, touching the overturned table with his foot, glancing upstairs.*)

Three times have I not been able to afford my partner any assistance—the dystentery, the smallpox, and now—

(HE *stares back at his chair, searching now into himself.*)

Of that ambition which has power for its object, I don't believe I have a spark in my heart. But is not the heart deceitful above all things?

(ABIGAIL *screams in labor in the dark above;* HE *is rigid.*)

I wait with impatience for the post!

(MAN 1 *comes with a letter toward* JOHN's *room;* JOHN *hurries to take it,* MAN 1 *retires,* JOHN *begins it with joy.*)

"Sir. The day before yesterday Mrs. Adams was delivered of a daughter; it grieves me to add that it was—stillborn. It was an exceedingly fine-looking child. Mrs. Adams—is as comfortable as can—"

(HE *cannot read on, sits on a step, averted.*

In the half-dark, the CHILDREN *come silently on to watch, as above, the* WOMEN *rise from* ABIGAIL; THEY *descend, one cradling a burden in her arms, and* THEY *bear it off; the* CHILDREN *go silently after.*

Faint light comes on ABIGAIL.)

ABIGAIL: About an hour ago I received a letter beginning, My dearest friend; one expression of that kind will—play about my heart—

(SHE *stands, unsteady.*)

I was as perfectly sensible of its decease as I before was of its existence. It appeared to be a very fine babe, and as it never opened its eyes on this world it looked as though they were only closed for sleep.

JOHN (*Racked*): My best friend. Is it not unaccountable that one should feel so for an infant that one has never seen?
The world is a riddle; long suffering is the lesson taught here. They say I am vain; vanity is the drop which makes the bitter cup of life go down.

(ABIGAIL *sits on her top step.*)

ABIGAIL: My heart was much set upon a daughter.
JOHN: When, oh when shall I see you again, and live in peace?

This day completes three years since I stepped into
the coach to Philadelphia, three years devoted to
liberty, a slavery to me. The loss of your company
I consider as a loss of so much solid happiness.
I want my talkative wife.

ABIGAIL (*Castles in the air*): If you will come home
and turn farmer, I will be dairy woman; our boys
shall go into the field and work with you, and my
girl stay in the house and assist me—

JOHN (*Likewise*): Let the cymbals of popularity tinkle,
let the butterflies of fame glitter with their wings,
I shall envy neither the music nor the colors—

ABIGAIL: —and we shall grow wealthy—

(*A great clanging of a bell shatters the dark, day-
light returns,* JOHN *starts to his feet; the* DELEGATES
*run in and converge down left—"Howe" is down
left, "Burgoyne" is up right—and* JOHN *is with
them, staring out. The bell, spaced at intervals,
continues.*

The MAP *again shows two fronts:* (1) *the British
sea arrow out of New York and up Chesapeake
Bay aimed at Philadelphia;* (2) *the British land
arrow aimed from Ticonderoga at Albany.*)

JOHN: It is now no secret where Howe's fleet is!

(ABIGAIL *comes downstairs, wanders.*)

ABIGAIL: I want a companion at nights, I often feel the
    want of your presence and affection—
JOHN (*Overlapping*): It is at the head of Chesapeake
    Bay, two hundred and sixty-three sail. There can
    be no doubt that he aims at this place.
ABIGAIL: Is this weakness? When I look around me—
MAN 1: Washington and his light horse came into town
    last night.
MAN 2: His army will be in this day.
MAN 3: Congress have ordered Gates to the north—

(JOHN *wheels back to center, staring at the* MAP
and up right; MAN 3 *follows him.*)

JOHN: Burgoyne I hope will be checked. He is a wild
    man, and will rush into—some measures which will
    put him in our power—
ABIGAIL: My habitation, how disconsolate it looks—
MAN 2: If Howe should get over the Brandywine—
JOHN (*Back to him*): —then Congress will remove. We
    now have an army between us and Mr. Howe.
ABIGAIL: —my table, I sit down to it, but cannot swallow
    my food. I cannot—

(*The* MEN *disperse;* JOHN *remains looking out,
then makes for his room.*)

—not give utterance to how much I have suffered
from this appearance of—inattention. When you
are wounded, I bleed—

JOHN (*Wildly*): For God's sake, never reproach me again with not writing! You know not the dangers which surround me or our country; I never wrote more letters, God knows I don't spend my time in gazing at curiosities!

(ABIGAIL *stands, blanching.*)

We live in critical moments; *this city is the stake for which the game is played!*

(*If used before, the shadow of a noose again dominates the* MAP.

Amid the bell strokes, a drum beat begins and ABIGAIL *turns;* JOHN *is on his steps, staring left.*)

ABIGAIL (*Alarmed*): Best of friends—
JOHN: *Will* Washington attack?

(*Down left sounds of gunfire begin, and mount.*)

ABIGAIL (*Excited*): From the southward—
JOHN: The battle of—the Brandywine!

(*For a few seconds the lights flicker upon them, like summer lightning, then all sounds abruptly cease.*)

Congress will remove!

(HE *runs up to his room, gathers up his bag, the*
lights dying on him. Total darkness, sounds of
running and blundering—in the blackout the GROUP
moves the platforms, JOHN'S *to up right,* ABIGAIL'S
to center—and a military trumpet, piercing; ABI-
GAIL'S *voice cries out from up left.*)

ABIGAIL: I know not where to write you. I heard the
enemy were in possession of Philadelphia—

(MEN 1 *and* 2 *enter down left as British* SOLDIERS
with a lantern, searching the empty hall; one boots
JOHN'S *chair away, the other sets up the royal flag*
again.

THEY *stand on guard, backs to us; thunder, the*
rattle of rain, and lightning reveals JOHN *on the*
platform up right.)

JOHN: York, Pennsylvania. Where will the light spring
up? From whence is our deliverance to come? Or
is it not to come? *Is the cause lost?*

(*From up left* ABIGAIL *comes in the lightning to*
center, seeing the SOLDIERS, *circling them.*)

ABIGAIL: Since the commencement of this war, by ways
and means the most improbable, Providence has
given into our hands those things we were in the
greatest necessity for—

(*Sounds of war commence again, behind* JOHN.)

JOHN: We have been in a state of tormenting uncertainty concerning the northward—

ABIGAIL: We have their armies *from* their shipping—tis what we have long sought, Heaven has granted us our desire—

JOHN: Letters—one-fifth of Burgoyne's forces destroyed at Bennington—

(*The sounds of battle rise.*)

Let New England cut off his retreat!

(HE *shouts above the thunder and the battle.*)

Now is the time to strike! Now is the time to destroy Burgoyne's gang root and branch! *New Englandmen, strike home!*

(*Now every conceivable sound breaks loose on-stage and throughout the house, cannon, trumpets, thunder, fifes, rifle fire, bells, in a red burning, with glimpses in lightning of* WOMEN *fleeing and* SOL-DIERS *running, a confusion of battle in which only* JOHN *is stationary; then all sound dies away.*

The MAP *shows the British arrow above Albany completely encircled.*

JOHN, *alone in a creeping of battlesmoke, whispers:*)
News I am afraid to write—

(*At rear, the* GROUP *regathers;* JOHN's *whisper is ecstatic.*)

—which lifted us up to the stars—
MEN, WOMEN:
Saratoga, '77.

(THEY *come down, survey the terrain.*)

Here,
October woodlands burning
Bright as bloodstains, a royal army lost,
This war, not done,
Comes at last to its turning.

France must open its ear.

(*The red light is paling out;* ABIGAIL *comes down, left.*)

ABIGAIL: General Burgoyne and his troops arrived last
week at Boston, humbled to the dust.
Now, my dear friend, a question I have not asked
for these ten months. This day completes thirteen
years since we were united in wedlock; three I have
lived in a state of widowhood—

(*The* MEN *and* WOMEN *come between them, arguing
with* JOHN.)

MEN, WOMEN:
     France must open its ear.
     This war, not done,
     Drinks
     Ships, arms, money, men;
     Five years more
     The blood will run,
     Southward, seaward;
     This war
     Is only begun.

(THEY *stand, waiting; then* JOHN *shakes his head.*)

JOHN: I was born to be in such times, but not made for
     them.
     Braintree, Braintree—Let me have my farm, family,
     and goosequill, and all the offices the world has to
     bestow may go to others; I court them not. My view
     is to lay fast hold of the town of Braintree and
     embrace it with both my arms, there to live, there
     to die, there to lay my bones.
     I am bound home.

(HE *retires;* MAN 3 *gives* ABIGAIL *a letter.*)

MAN 3 : From the Congress.

ABIGAIL: Your letter comes to my hand in the absence
of Mr. Adams—

(SHE *reads it.*)

Oh, sir—

(HER *dismay grows.*)

I know you mean the public good, or—how could
you contrive to rob me of all my happiness?

(JOHN *comes down;* SHE *surrenders the letter and*
HE *reads it.*)

JOHN: "Your domestic happiness was not consulted,
but the necessity of your country for your talents.
We want one man of inflexible integrity on that
embassy—in France—"

MAN 3:
       To ask
       Ships, arms, money, men,
       Is the task;
       France will open its ear
       To you.
JOHN: *France?*

(HE *stares at* ABIGAIL, *at the* CHILDREN, *at the*
letter.)

ABIGAIL (*Finally*): Life takes its complexion from—
   inferior things—

   (SHE *means herself, the house, the* CHILDREN; SHE
   waits upon his decision.)

   Only a few years are our portion, who shall com-
   pensate to me those years? Give me the man I
   love. I know the voice of fame to be a mere—
   weathercock—

   (SHE *waits;* HE *is silent.*)

   I consider the honors with which you are invested
   as badges of my unhappiness!
JOHN (*Low*): And do you so soon forget?
ABIGAIL (*An outcry*): Who shall give me back time?

   (*A pause.*)

WOMEN (*Softly*):
   None,
   When the war is won
   And the weather washes the dream
   Out of the places—

   (THEY *begin to divest themselves of costume now,
   scrap by scrap, returning completely into the
   present.*)

JOHN (*To* THEM): And do *you* so soon forget the ground where liberty was fought for?

(ABIGAIL *turns, sits averted;* HE *speaks to her back, to the* OTHERS.)

No nation has long enjoyed that—imperfect emancipation we call a free government; frivolities and military glories, luxuries and lies, sooner or later undermine all principles. We are not a chosen people, we must and shall go the way of the earth.

MEN, WOMEN (*Softly*):
Look at this country, this
Is the theme—

JOHN (*Overriding*): We ought to swim, though, against the wind and the tide as long as we can, to amend —humanity—

(*To the* CHILDREN.)

—invent new medicines, construct new machines, write new books, institute better governments—be sensible of each other's ignorance, weakness, and error—

(*To the* OTHERS *and us.*)

Tell your neighbors and children that this is holy ground, holier than that on which your churches stand!

(HE *comes behind* ABIGAIL, *touches her.*)

The human universe is asleep; it must awake.

(*Long pause.* ABIGAIL *sits in misery.*)

ABIGAIL: Alas, my dear, I am much afflicted with a disorder called the heartache, nor can any remedy be found.

JOHN (*Presently*): I wonder whether anybody but you would believe me sincere if I were to say how much I love you, and wish to be with you, never to be separated more?

(HE *waits on her consent; and at last* SHE *bows to it.*)

ABIGAIL: My thoughts are fixed, my latest wish depends on thee, guide, guardian, husband, lover, friend.

(HE *begins to move back from her; the* BOY *comes to him,* JOHN *catches his hand.*)

JOHN: I shall certainly return home in the spring.

ABIGAIL: Difficult as the day is—cruel as this war has been—

JOHN: With or without leave, home I will come!

ABIGAIL: —separated as I am on account of it from the dearest connection in life—

JOHN: So, wait—

ABIGAIL: —my first choice would be the same—

JOHN: —wait—

ABIGAIL: —if I again had youth to make it.

JOHN: —wait to receive your old friend, J. Adams.

(HE *and the* BOY *go out among the* GROUP.

ABIGAIL *sits and waits; and around her the* OTHERS *commence to take the set apart, as the lights die out on her and on them.*)

WILLIAM GIBSON

William Gibson, who was born in New York City in 1914, and who now lives in Stockbridge, Massachusetts, with his wife and two sons, has previously written four plays which have been produced in New York, Dinny and the Witches, Two for the Seesaw, The Miracle Worker, *and* A Cry of Players; *a novel,* The Cobweb; *a volume of poetry,* Winter Crook; *a theater chronicle,* The Seesaw Log; *and a family chronicle,* A Mass for the Dead.